Long Distance Hiking
on the
Appalachian Trail
for the Older Adventurer

Long Distance Hiking on the Appalachian Trail

for the Older Adventurer

David Ryan

NEW MOUNTAIN BOOKS

Long Distance Hiking on the Appalachian Trail for the Older Adventurer © 2002 by David Ryan

ALL RIGHTS RESERVED

FIRST EDITION 2002
10 9 8 7 6 5 4 3

LIBRARY OF CONGRESS CATALOG CARD NUMBER: 2002103021
ISBN: 0–938631–20–9 paper

PHOTOGRAPHS: David Ryan

BOOK DESIGN/PRODUCTION:
V. S. Elliott, SunFlower Designs of Santa Fe
TYPEFACES: Minion, Benguiat Gothic

PUBLISHED BY:

NEW MOUNTAIN BOOKS
13233 Executive Ridge Dr., NE
Albuquerque, New Mexico 87112
www.newmountainbooks.com

Contents

Preface

There seems to be much emphasis in the outdoor sports media on extreme adventure — typically available only to the very fit, the very rich and the very crazy. Focus is given to adrenaline junkies of all ages zooming over 100 miles per hour on their motorcycles, rushing through class five rapids in their kayaks or dangling precariously hundreds of feet in the air from the edge of a cliff. This is exciting and wonderful, but what about the rest of us? There are people in their middle years and older who are ready to take on challenges other than their careers. They are not ready to let their bellies turn to jelly and are not content to ride around in a golf cart or lean back in a recliner and watch television all day. They are not looking for a pre-programmed tour nor are they content to let the Disney Corporation interpret the world for them. They are looking for an adventure that can be achieved by someone of reasonable strength and condition, an experience that will not kill them in the process and a journey that can be managed without breaking the bank. Long distance hiking is an adventure that fits all of those criteria. Rather than raw strength and athleticism, it takes stamina and perseverance. Rather than the adrenaline rush of a near death experience, it offers serenity and contemplation. It is an activity that can be done on your own for no more cost than normal living expenses. This publication has been written by an older adventurer for those who are no longer young and would like to take on the adventure of a long distance hike.

CHAPTER
ONE

Deciding to Hike

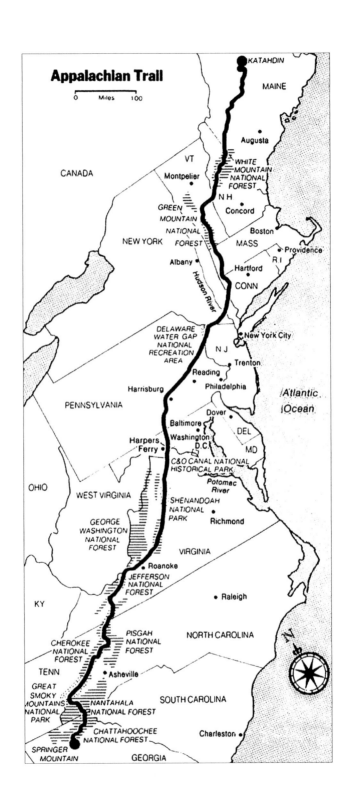

LONG DISTANCE HIKING

If you go by the advertisements and articles in outdoor sport and hiking magazines, you would expect that every long distance hiker is extraordinarily fit, athletic and muscular. Not all, and perhaps few, long distance hikers actually fit this profile. Long distance hikers come in all shapes and ages. Surprisingly, there are many older adventurers (middle age and older) pursuing their dreams on long distance hiking paths. This publication is intended to assist those older adventurers who are planning, contemplating, or just curious about long distance hiking. It is not a replacement for a comprehensive guide on backpacking or a specific trail guidebook, but rather meant to be a good resource for pointing you in the right direction for the information you need to have for a successful long distance hike. For purposes of this discussion, a long distance hike is a hike long enough to remove you from your normal routine and to force you to adopt a completely different life-style. This is a hike well in excess of a month's duration. An example is a thru-hike (end to end) or a substantial section of a long distance hiking trail (Appalachian Trail, Continental Divide Trail, Pacific Crest Trail or other).

For those of you not familiar with those trails, the Appalachian Trail runs from Georgia to Maine along the crest of the Appalachian Mountains. It is the oldest of the long distance hiking trails. The Pacific Crest Trail starts at the Mexican border and follows the Sierra Nevada and Cascade Mountains through California, Oregon and Washington to the Canadian border. The Continental Divide Trail is a newer trail that is still under development. It runs on or near the Continental Divide from Mexico to Canada through New Mexico and the Rocky Mountains.

There are many people in their late forties, fifties, sixties and even seventies taking long distance hikes. Some are retirees, others are in a period of transition and others may be taking a break from the work world. One hiker I met was a legally blind man in his fifties who was doing as much hiking as he could before his eyesight completely left him. The one thing all older adventurers have in common is that they arranged their lives to have sufficient time to complete a long distance hike. In many ways the older hiker has an advantage over the younger in successfully achieving their goal. The older hiker is more likely to have enough maturity and personal security not to be distracted by temptations along the way and actually to enjoy and thrive in a world of lower stimulation and calm. The older hiker has had enough life experience to value and appreciate the opportunity to live life differently. The hard knocks and lessons of life have provided the older adventurer the focus and durability that will serve well in a long distance hike.

If you have done much reading about hiking, you have probably been entertained by the misadventures of Bill Bryson and his friend Katz in Bryson's best selling book *A Walk in the Woods: Rediscovering America on the Appalachian Trail.* If you are serious about meeting your expectations, Bill Bryson is not the example you want to follow. If you have read his book, you know that he gave up on his long distance hike after walking 200 miles. Two hundred miles may sound like a lot, but it was over 1,900 miles short of his goal of thru-hiking the Appalachian Trail. It is too bad that he switched gears at 200 miles because the 200-mile mark is when novice hikers have finally mastered their outdoor skills and have hiked their bodies into good condition. If you are able to hike 200 miles, you have the physical ability to hike 400 miles, 1,000 miles or the 2,160 miles of the entire Appalachian Trail. After 200 miles, long distance hiking switches from being a physical challenge to being a mental challenge. To make it to that first 200 miles will require good preparation, good attitude, good humor and adaptability.

I completed hiking the Appalachian Trail two days after my fifty-first birthday. My wife and I had started the trail the year before but had to cut our adventure short when she broke her leg. The next year when we resumed our hike, she had to stop after a couple of weeks because her leg was still weak. I continued hiking and made it to the end, while my wife joined up with me with the car and drove on roads near the trail as I hiked. In that way we were able to camp out at night together and share the experience.

My wife and I came to thru-hiking the Appalachian Trail by way of a Civil War soldier's diary. The diary noted a hot spring in western North Carolina, and we decided to check it out on our next vacation. When we visited Hot Springs, North Carolina, we found out that the Appalachian Trail passed right through the middle of town. We hiked along the trail for a mile or two and liked what we saw. When we went back to town we bought some books about the trail.

The timing for our discovering the Appalachian Trail was perfect. We had been seriously planning to simplify our lives and leave the full time work world. We were also looking for challenging and fulfilling activities for our upcoming free time. We continued our research and added thru-hiking the Appalachian Trail to the list of adventures we would pursue.

DECIDING TO DO A LONG DISTANCE HIKE

The first consideration of taking a long distance hike is to understand why you want to do it. It may be as simple as having a good time, or something that you have always wanted to do. It could be as involved as a "vision quest", or a period of contemplation during a time of transition, grief or adjustment. For us, we wanted simplicity and clarity. The trail answered both of those desires. You cannot get simpler than living on what you can carry on your back and nothing can be more clear than the need to pack up each morning and step out. We also achieved a great sense of accomplishment. Our goal was to step on the trail in Georgia and hike until we stepped off in Maine. Unlike much of what we did in the work world, we were no longer pushing air and accomplishing little. We could see how many miles we covered in a day. We could tell that we were getting stronger by the increased miles, by the reduced effort it took to go uphill and the fewer aches we had at night. You know you have arrived when you look more forward to going uphill than going downhill.

Best of all we achieved a sense of being in the present. We were not concerned with regrets, worry or anticipations. We were not being bombarded with negative imagery: television, newspapers, traffic, deadlines or demands. We were immersed in the natural world. We were just here, in the present, living out of our backpack and adding to our miles. It is when you are in the present that you have the ability to see, to appreciate all that is around you and just be thankful for what you have been offered. The opportunity to see all the leaves, the roots, the creatures—large and small, the light, the breeze, the smells, how every day is different and to realize that it all works, and that you are here with it is something that you will be thankful for the rest of your life. As one hiking colleague told me, it was the best thing he had ever done for himself.

DECIDING WHERE TO DO A LONG DISTANCE HIKE

Enough about why hike; the next task is to choose where to hike. I may be prejudiced from thru-hiking the Appalachian Trail, but I have also hiked portions of both the Pacific Crest Trail and Continental Divide Trail. I have even adopted a small portion of the Continental Divide Trail in New Mexico. Despite that, for the older adventurer considering a long distance hike, I recommend the Appalachian Trail.

All three trails have difficult hiking. Some claim that the Appalachian Trail, despite its lower elevations, may have the hardest hiking. This is because many trails in the West have been graded to accommodate pack animals. The Appalachian Trail does not have pack animals and in many sections the trail shoots straight up without a switchback. Local clubs who are responsible for trail maintenance have gone out of their way to make their particular section memorable. If you look closely at a trail map you can see how the trail seems to meander to catch every peak, knob or crest. When Earl Shaffer, the first person to hike the trail end to end in 1948, hiked the trail again in 1998 to commemorate the fiftieth anniversary of his first thru-hike, he complained that the trail was too hard. It may be because he was seventy-nine or that the Appalachian Trail is tough.

I will concede that both the Pacific Crest and Continental Divide Trails have more sweeping vistas, but the Appalachian Trail is not absent of views. Even though the Appalachian Trail parallels the eastern seaboard and passes within an hour's drive of many populous metropolitan areas, there is a feeling of being in rugged remote country. The main reasons that the older hiker should choose the Appalachian Trail over the other trails are **water** and **resupply.** The Pacific Crest and Continental Divide Trail have long stretches in the desert where reliable water sources can be up to 20 miles or more apart. This means that you have to be able to carry a gallon or two of water with you and be able to hike 20 miles per day immediately from the beginning of the hike. Very few hikers, regardless of their age, will be capable of this.

The amount of water you will need to carry in the desert is way too much weight for a sensible long distance hike — especially for the older hiker. The lack of water probably means leaving the dog at home. This could lead to one very ornery and disappointed dog. Many who do hike in the desert on a regular basis cache (store) water along their planned route. This is quite sensible for a short duration hike, but it is not practical for a thru-hike. A thru-hike requires that you have the ability to sustain yourself as you go along your journey of several weeks and hundreds of miles.

Resupplying yourself along the way means needing access to towns for taking a shower, doing laundry, picking up mail and buying supplies. Although the Appalachian Trail actually only passes directly through a few towns, there are services at many of the road crossings, and there are usually towns only a few miles away when you reach a crossing. Because local residents are used to seeing hikers at road crossings, getting a ride to town is usually very easy. Appalachian Trail thru-hikers should be able to resupply themselves, except in a few cases, every three to five days. This frequency of resupply is not possible on either the Pacific Crest or Continental Divide Trails. This means that the Pacific Crest and Continental Divide Trail hiker must be able to hike faster and/or carry more weight between resupply points.

Some "man in the wilderness types" will argue that the Appalachian Trail is too crowded and does not offer the solitude they are seeking. There are certainly other hikers on the Appalachian Trail, but in most cases they are spread out and for much of the day on the trail you will not see another hiker. Even if several people are camping at the same location as you, it is most likely that each party will leave at a different time. Once someone makes a turn they will be out of sight and you will have the trail to yourself. The only places where the Appalachian Trail is crowded are in some of the National Parks, the White Mountains in New Hampshire and on occasional weekends. Crowds, if present, typically thin out quickly.

Having fellow hikers on the trail is not necessarily a bad thing. Why should volunteers, organizations and agencies build and maintain a trail that will not be used? Is it so bad to meet people along the trail who understand what you are doing and can share in the experience? This shared experience creates a very tight and generally positive community on the trail. If you need help, it is nice to know that there is a community ready to help you. My wife and I are extremely grateful for the help provided by other hikers in getting her off the trail, when she broke her leg five miles from the nearest road crossing. I would hate to think what it would be like to be on a remote trail in New Mexico with a broken leg, baking in the desert, without water or other hikers to help. Again, there are many great trails for hiking, but for the older long distance adventurer going on a hike that will be measured in months, the Appalachian Trail is the best choice.

CHAPTER TWO

Before the Hike

RESEARCHING YOUR HIKE

A thru-hike of the Appalachian Trail will take five to seven months (five-and-one-half to six months are average). If you do not have six months available or do not want to devote six months to a hike, a two or three month section hike will give you a good long distance hiking experience. Because you will be investing a considerable amount of time and resources to this adventure it makes sense that you learn something about the trail before starting your journey.

You should involve yourself in the trail by joining the Appalachian Trail Conference (ATC)—the organization that manages the trail. Without the ATC we would not be having this discussion. In addition to making the trail possible, the ATC is a good source for information and books on the trail. The ATC can be reached at:

Appalachian Trail Conference
799 Washington Street, PO Box 807
Harpers Ferry, West Virginia 25425
(304) 535–6331 • www.atconf.org

The Appalachian Trail has a fascinating history and a unique culture. Bill Bryson mentions in his book that the Appalachian Trail has been used longer than the Santa Fe Trail, Oregon Trail or Route 66 were used. There are many books that can provide you a good background on the trail. Two that I recommend are:

➤ *A Walk in the Woods*, by Bill Bryson — (1998)
     terrible for planning, but very funny and great background,
and
➤ *Walking the Appalachian Trail*, by Larry Luxenberg —
    (1994) good history and background on the trail culture

Both books can be ordered from the ATC.

You will also need specific information on the trail for planning your hike and for carrying with you on the trail. Three publications essential for the hike are:

➤ *The Thru-Hiker's Handbook*, by Dan "Wingfoot" Bruce
➤ *Appalachian Trail Data Book* published by the ATC
➤ *Appalachian Trail Maps* published by the ATC

The Thru-Hiker's Handbook is published annually by the Center for Appalachian Trail Studies, which is the author's organization, and can be ordered from Amazon.com, or the author's website — www.trailplace.com. The Handbook has information on shelters and where to camp along the trail, post office locations and services available in towns near the trail. Those services include where to buy fuel for your camp stove, where to stay (hostels, motels...), grocery stores and the like. The information on towns is critical for sustaining your hike. A similar guide is published by the Appalachian Long

Distance Hiker's Association (ALDHA) and can be purchased from the ATC. The "Wingfoot" book is the most widely used by thru-hikers.

The Appalachian Trail Data Book, which is published annually, provides the mileage points for shelters, campsites, springs, road crossings, and towns. This information is essential for daily planning while on the trail. When you need to know how far it is to water or to the next road, this is the book to use. This book can be purchased from the ATC.

The Appalachian Trail Maps, which are updated every now and then, are companions to the eleven volume Appalachian Trail Guide set. The guide set is not critical for your hike or planning. It is a nice to have rather than a need to have. **The maps are a need to have.** The maps not only show the trail route; they also have elevation profiles for the trail. Both the route and profile information are important for daily planning. The maps and guides can be purchased from the ATC. If you buy the guides, the maps are included at no additional charge. To save money on purchasing guides, the ATC has an annual clearance sale of the previous year's guides every fall.

If you are fairly new to hiking, or a complete novice, you will want to learn something about hiking. There are many general books on hiking available at your nearest bookstore. I found Trailside: Hiking and Backpacking—A Complete Guide by Karen Berger (1995) to be very helpful. You will want to test some of your basic skills before hitting the trail. My wife and I almost started a forest fire the first time we lit our backpacking stove. We did not realize that we had coated the picnic table where we had set up the stove with fuel when we were priming the stove. When we lit the fuel the entire picnic table turned into a fireball and flames were leaping over ten feet into the air. Fortunately, it had been very rainy and the table was waterlogged so the flames quickly burned out. You do not want to conduct that type of experiment on the trail (or anywhere else if possible).

GENERAL PLANNING

The Appalachian Trail runs a 2,160 course from Springer Mountain in north Georgia to Mount Katahdin in north central Maine. The trail tends to run southwest to northeast. Most thru-hikers start their trek in Georgia in March or April and work their way north. A Georgia start makes it possible to finish the hike between late August and mid-October well before winter settles in on Mount Katahdin. If you begin in Maine you will have to wait for the snow to clear and the blackflies to die off. This usually means starting in June. With a start this late, you will be rolling the dice on finishing before winter.

Climate is another advantage that the Appalachian Trail has over both the Pacific Crest and Continental Divide Trails. Do not get me wrong—you **will** have severe weather on the Appalachian Trail, but you will be able to make uninterrupted and continuous progress. This is very iffy on both the Pacific Crest and Continental Divide Trails. On those trails you will have to clear the southern deserts in April. By May the deserts will be too hot and too exposed for most older hikers to enjoy. After clearing the deserts you will then have high altitude (over 10,000 feet) mountains. You may then have to wait until late June, or later, for the snow to melt in the highest elevations. This could mean hop-scotching around in order to keep moving, or hovering while waiting for the snow to melt. It will take an extraordinary hiker with snow gear to make continuous progress in one direction on the Pacific Crest or Continental Divide Trails.

A mid-April snow in the Smokies briefly slowed but did not impede hiking—Rocky Top Mountain, Tennessee *is ahead.*

For your hike of the Appalachian Trail you will want to make some sort of a general plan. The purpose of the general plan is to give you an idea of where you expect to be at various stages of the journey. This will help in planning off-trail activities such as visits with friends, determining where it will be possible to switch to warm weather gear and identifying likely resupply points. It is not necessary to micro-manage a six month hike ahead of time, and it will probably be a wasted effort because there will be plenty of changes along the way.

The best way to develop a general plan is to use the maps, Handbook and Data Book to plot where you expect to be each week. For the older hiker I recommend that you schedule a full rest day every seven to ten days. You will need the rest, and you will need time to do laundry, resupply and catch up. Earlier in the hike those rest days should be closer together— perhaps, at least five days and no more than seven days apart. Later in the hike, when you are stronger, a full day of rest could come every ten days with intermittent half-day stops for re-supply. Your body will tell you when to rest, and if you are wise, you will listen.

If you are not an Olympian, plan on starting your hike slowly. There are plenty of places for water and resupply along the Appalachian Trail so there is no need to force yourself to go faster than you are ready to go. The trail is much harder than anyone expects. Taking it easy in the first days of hiking will allow your body to harden. This will give you the strength to make it to the end. The first nights on the trail will be nights of aches. You will wake up wondering if you are a teenager again with growing pains in your legs. As your body hardens the aches will go away and the need to take aspirin or ibuprofen will become a distant memory. If you do not take it easy and choose to go out too fast there is a very good likelihood that you will hurt yourself, or burn out, and leave the trail well before reaching your goal.

For planning purposes, seven or eight miles a day for the first week or two is a very good average. Based upon five and half days of hiking that would be 40 or 45 miles for the first week. For the second week, if you are ready, I would raise the average to ten miles per day, or 55 miles for the week. In the third week, again if you are ready, I would up the average again to twelve miles per day, or close to 70 miles for the week. That may remain a good average for you for the entire hike and would keep you on the trail for seven months. Some of you will raise you average to well over 100 miles per week and finish the hike in five or six months. Because New Hampshire and Maine are more rugged, you will need to reduce your expected average by at least 30 to 35 percent or more. That is, if you are hiking 80 miles a week, plan on 50 to 60 miles a week or fewer. Some weeks will even be slower.

Starting at Amicalola Falls State Park, Georgia *on a very cool day in March with a very overloaded pack.*

WHAT TO CARRY ON THE TRAIL

Once you have used your expected pace to create a general plan, it is time to determine what to take along. The weight in your pack is crucial to how well you will hike. Less is better. Reducing your pack weight will enable you to increase your average miles and will make climbing hills easier. I started my hike with over 65 pounds, and it was staggering. When I put my pack down, I felt like I had to grab a branch to keep from floating away. I quickly got the pack weight down to 50 pounds and eventually pared it down to around 35 to 40 pounds depending upon the amount of food I was carrying. Even that is heavy, but it is so much better than 65 pounds.

I saw many people, some with injuries, leave the trail in the first few miles because they were carrying too much weight. On the very first day, as I was trudging up Springer Mountain, I was almost run over by a mother and her grown daughter storming down the mountain. They were not talking to each other and were close to tears because they could not handle the weight. When I reached the top, another man who was pitching his tent said, "tomorrow I am getting off the trail because if I am going to carry this much weight, I'd rather carry a set of golf clubs and go around the country checking out golf courses."

If you can make it 30 miles further up the trail, there is help for overweight packs, tight boots and poorly performing equipment—The Walisi-Yi Center. This is an outfitter and re-supply center staffed with experts on long distance hiking. The trail actually goes through their building. They are better than a crisis center and have rescued many hikes. If your pack is heavy, they will help you identify items to take out of your pack and send home. If you have the wrong gear, they can sell you the gear you need. If your boots are tight, they can replace your insoles and sell you thinner socks. They rescued our hike by helping us eliminate blisters and reduce pack weight.

Before examining what should or should not go into your pack, it is important to talk about your boots. Boots, as much as pack weight, are a major source of discomfort on the trail. Make sure your boots fit correctly and are broken in. Boots are not supposed to be tight. They are supposed to be comfort-able. Your boots need to broken in by carrying a backpack, not just hiking, before you start the hike. The trail, as we found out, is not the place to realize that you have a boot problem. Fortunately, the Walisi-Yi Center was able to help us out. Once you have your boots right, the walking will be much better and you can now focus on your pack weight.

There are as many theories on pack weight as there are hikers. A popular theory making the rounds today is "ultra light" hiking. Many of the advocates of ultra light hiking are Olympian athletes who think nothing of hiking 35 miles a day and completing the Appalachian Trail in three months. I do not think many older hikers will fall into this category. Ultra light techniques, if used improperly, can be dangerous. Keeping the pack weight down is important, but it is also important to be adequately prepared. Perhaps, I am an advocate of "light" rather than "ultra light." It is important to examine everything that goes into your pack and determine if it should be there. One good rule, which you will read in every hiking guide, is that if you are not using something regularly, it does not belong in your pack unless it is for emergencies such as a first aid kit.

Lists of what to bring on a long distance hike can be found in most books on hiking and backpacking. Items that you need to hike the Appalachian Trail are listed here for your review. The items with an asterisk (*) are described in greater detail.

BACKPACK
Rain Cover for backpack

SLEEPING BAG*
Sleeping Pad*

TENT* and **GROUND CLOTH**

CLOTHING*
Rain Gear
Winter Clothes
Summer Clothes
Camp Shoes

BOOTS* and **SOCKS**

WATER PURIFICATION*
Filter

Spare Filter Cartridge
Iodine Tablets

WATER BOTTLES*

FOOD*

COOKING EQUIPMENT*
Stove
Fuel
Pot
Liquid Soap
Pot Scrubber
Utensils
Lighter or Matches

PERSONAL HYGIENE
Wash Cloth
Camp Towel
Face Soap
Tooth Brush, Tooth Paste and Dental Floss
Deodorant*
Treatments (for skin, athletes feet)
Pain Medicine
Personal Medicine
Insect Repellent*
Sunscreen*
Toilet Paper
Trowel for burying waste
Waterless hand soap

UTILITY ITEMS
Rope — for hanging food, drying clothes and other uses
First Aid Kit

Compass*
Whistle
Multi Purpose Knife (Swiss Army Knife)
Small Flash Light (pen light)
Repair Tools*
Duct Tape—wrapped around a water bottle
Replacement and Maintenance Items (batteries,
    bootlaces, boot wax, equipment parts)

BUSINESS ITEMS
Handbook pages, Data Book pages, Maps*
Journal and Pen—you will want to keep track of
    your journey
Camera and Film
Reading Material*
Business Materials*

WALKING STICK, GLOVES, BANDANNA and HAT

Items that I recommend you **not** take include:

GPS DEVICE—you just do not need one on the
    Appalachian Trail

CANDLE LANTERN and **EXTRA CANDLES***

CAMP CHAIR—it's nice, but it is weight that you
    do not need

BINOCULARS—their weight is more than their
    usefulness

A word of advice on whatever gear you get is to make sure
that it is durable. You do not want your gear to break down on
the trail. Also when you buy gear from an outfitter, make sure

that the person giving you advice knows what he or she is talking about. When you enter the store tell them that you are planning a long distance hike and ask them if they have any experienced long distance hikers on staff. If they do, they may be able to give you some valuable tips.

Before going to an outfitter, it would make sense to research the equipment you intend to buy. *Backpacker* magazine regularly reviews equipment and publishes an annual "Gear Guide" every March (available in February). The reviews and gear guide compare equipment and include essential information on durability, price, and weight. Equipment reviews are also available on the *Backpacker* magazine web site www.backpacker.com.

SLEEPING BAG

Some ultra light advocates claim that you can wear all of your clothes when you go to sleep and get along without a sleeping bag or with only a lightweight bag. If you are doing a thru-hike, you will most likely be starting your hike in late March or early April. At that time of the year the lower elevations of the South are in full spring with balmy weather and dogwoods in bloom. On the Appalachian Trail, it is still late winter without even a bud showing. It is cold at night, and it can go well below freezing and even snow.

One hiking companion tried sleeping without a bag. He put on all of his clothes, zipped them up tight and put on a knit wool cap. It was the last day of March, and it had been cool that day. That night the bottom fell out and the temperature dropped into the low twenties. The only thing that kept him from freezing to death was the willingness of a very large dog to sleep on him. The next day he was the first one out of camp to hurry to the nearest town and buy a sleeping bag. End of experiment.

If you are starting in March or April you will want a warm sleeping bag (rated for 20 degrees) on the Appalachian Trail. Because it also gets wet on the trail, you are better off with a bag with synthetic fill rather than down fill. A down bag will lose its insulating powers when wet. When buying a sleeping bag with synthetic fill, make sure it is light in weight. You do not want a heavy bag that is suitable only for car camping or a sleepover. When the weather gets warmer in mid to late May, you can save pack weight by switching to a lighter weight summer sleeping bag. Also, if you are starting your hike later in the year, you may be able to get along only with a summer weight sleeping bag.

SLEEPING PAD

A sleeping pad is essential for protecting yourself from losing body heat to the ground. Even though outfitters offer a large array of large comfortable self-inflating sleeping pads, stay away from them. They are too heavy to take on the trail. Stick with a lightweight foam pad. Another plus a foam pad offers is that you will save the negligible weight of a repair kit for the self-inflating mattress.

TENT

The Appalachian Trail has shelters located at reasonable intervals from beginning to end. (Shelters are usually open three wall structures with a roof and a floor.) It would be possible to camp nearly every night at a shelter and not pack a tent. Even if you like and plan to sleep in a shelter every night, you

A newer and one of the nicer shelters on the trail near Mount Rogers, Virginia.

should carry a tent or equivalent. This is because a shelter may not be available when you are ready to stop, or the shelter may be full when you get there.

I would add to the argument — do you really want to sleep in a shelter? Shelters are great places to congregate. Other hikers will be there, and there is usually reliable water nearby. There are also registers in the shelters to enter notes to other hikers and to keep up with trail events. But for sleeping, shelters are much colder than a zipped up tent, less private and full of mice. You could spend much of the night being a landing pad for leaping mice while listening to your neighbors snore. However, shelters are great places during rainy weather. They negate the need to set up or break down a tent in the rain, and they will save you from carrying the extra pounds of a wet tent the next day.

Regardless of whether or not you like sleeping in shelters

a back-up shelter system is required. Some hikers have selected a bivey sack or a tarp as a lightweight alternative to a tent. For my tastes, the bivey sack is too claustrophobic and a tarp too open. I have been satisfied with carrying a lightweight tent.

CLOTHING

You will need rain protection on the Appalachian Trail. Springtime in the southern Appalachians is very rainy. During a five-week period while I was hiking the trail it rained sometime during the day on 30 out of 35 days. Sometimes it would be a brief shower, other times a deluge. Regardless, it was wet, and for both safety and comfort it is important to keep dry. This means a rain jacket and rain pants. It also means that all your clothes must be light, strong and quick drying. This means fleece, synthetics, and absolutely no cotton. As every hiking and backpacking publication stresses— cotton kills. Cotton is very heavy when wet; it is very cold when wet; and it takes forever to dry.

When the weather gets warmer, you can shed pack weight by getting rid of your heavy weight winter fleece and winter clothes. You may want to get rid of your rain pants as long as you keep your rain jacket and a lightweight fleece in case it rains or gets cool. If it rains, the rain jacket will keep your top dry and your synthetic shorts can be dried when you make camp. If you are cold, you can warm up in your sleeping bag. If you are concerned about not carrying a pair of rain pants, you can experiment by hiking without them before making a decision on sending them home. If you do get too cold, you should keep the pants. If you are fine without the rain pants, send them home.

Another clothing item where you can save weight are

camp shoes. Many people carry Tevas to wear around camp. I love Tevas and wear them as everyday footwear, but they are too heavy to carry in your pack. Lightweight thongs or shower shoes are better.

Boots

While on the subject of footwear, we need to get back to boots. There are two items to consider regarding boots. One is that you will most likely wear out one pair of boots on the trail, and the other is that lighter boots are easier for hiking. This means that you should have two pairs of boots broken in before starting the hike. I recommend that you wear a pair of lighter to mid-weight high-cut boots with waterproofing (ie, Gore-Tex) when the weather is colder and wetter (at the beginning of the hike). The other pair of boots could be a pair of low-cut hiking boots. Make sure that the soles on both pairs of boots have good traction on wet rocks and that the soles are strong enough to protect your feet bottoms from sharp rocks. I have found some low-cut boots to have poor traction and have cracked my skull more than once when slipping on wet rocks. Another pair of low-cut boots that I wore had very soft soles. I was able to feel every point of every rock. You may pick up a bit of weight, but you will appreciate a low-cut boot with a better sole. With two pairs of boots you can then swap them depending upon trail conditions. (This is discussed in greater detail later in "Sustaining the Hike" on page 39.)

Water Purification

Many hikers have gotten sick because they did not treat or filter their water. An ultra light hiker will use iodine tablets because they are much lighter than a water filter. I used a water filter because iodine not only kills what's in the water; it also kills what's in your stomach even those things that are good for you. Iodine is fine for short periods of time, but I am not sure I want to perform a six-month experiment of destroying intestinal microbes on myself. Water from a water filter also tastes better. I did reduce pack weight by not carrying a spare water filter cartridge. I carried iodine tablets as a lightweight back up. Boiling water is not a good option for the long distance hiker because it takes too much time and requires too much fuel (extra weight).

WATER BOTTLES

Bottles are another area to save weight. Many lightweight hikers have substituted their water bottles with light plastic beverage bottles. They are light and cheap to replace. Remember, on the Appalachian Trail, you will rarely need to carry more than one full bottle of water. You will need additional bottles for when you make camp, but those can remain empty until then.

FOOD AND COOKING EQUIPMENT

The heaviest variable items in your pack will be food and cooking gear. An immediate item you can get rid of to save weight is the second pot in your cook kit. One pot is sufficient. Another way to save weight is to cook only once a day. This will not only save clean up time — it will reduce the amount of fuel you need to carry. An 11 ounce (small) fuel bottle will be sufficient for a solo hiker. A hiking couple may need a larger 22 ounce bottle, or two 11 ounce fuel bottles. If you do not need that daily cup of coffee you could further reduce your pack weight by not cooking at all. You will no longer need your stove, fuel or cook kit.

Not being a coffee drinker, I was able to save considerable weight by going to cold food when I started hiking without my wife. In the morning my breakfast was powdered milk mixed with Instant Breakfast and water and a Pop Tart. Later in the morning I would have another Pop Tart or Cliff Bar (or equivalent) as a snack. Lunch would be peanut butter and honey on a bagel. In the afternoon I would have another snack (oatmeal cookie sandwich, candy bar or Pringles). When I finished hiking and made camp, I would mix up a quart of Gatorade and down it in one swallow. Dinner was a sandwich that I calculated to be 900 calories—a small 3 ounce can of Spam Spread and a slab of cheese on a large bagel. For dessert and throughout the day, I nibbled on gorp (good old raisins and peanuts—trail mix). I made gorp with oily cocktail peanuts, raisins and plain M&M's. I must tell you that those meals tasted great and that my health was never better.

You may be wondering why would I rave about a Spam sandwich and why would someone pick up and eat an M&M laying on the trail (this actually happened). When you are hiking day in day out through rugged country carrying a pack, you get hungry. I have read that you may be burning anywhere from 4,000 to 6,000 calories a day. It is very hard to carry or eat that much food. At some point on the trail your appetite will kick in and eating will become a major focus (or obsession). When you reach town pigging out will become an art form. It is not a cheeseburger and shake, but two cheeseburgers and two shakes. You will not want a light salad and vegetables; you will want the densest, most filling food you can find. You will be eating and living truly as a hunter/gatherer.

To a non-long distance hiker, the on-trail and off-trail

food regimen sounds less than optimal and, perhaps, unhealthy. The reality is that if you avoid fatigue and injuries you will be healthy regardless of what you eat for at least two reasons. One is that your contact with other people is limited; therefore, your exposure to colds and other illnesses is reduced. The other is that with continuous hiking your body is looking for calories and metabolizing everything that you eat. During that process your immune system has also kicked into overdrive to ward off illness. Perhaps, being outdoors in a positive environment with fresh air, away from stress, continuously exercising and drinking plenty of filtered water are other factors in keeping healthy.

A smart way to save on food weight is to buy sensibly. If your next replenishment stop is five days out, you do not need ten days worth of gorp. You only need five, or maybe six, days worth of gorp. When my wife and I started hiking we carried a heavy squeeze bottle of margarine for making macaroni and cheese. We soon realized that we could toss out the one pound margarine bottle and use tuna packed in oil to make the macaroni and cheese. We saved another pound when we replaced a large squeeze bottle of jelly with a small bottle of honey.

Increasing your daily average miles can also reduce your pack weight. The more miles that you can hike in a day the sooner you will reach a supply point. Instead of carrying five days worth of food, you might be able to reduce it to three days. Assuming two pounds of food per day, four pounds would be eliminated in your pack. (It is prudent to keep an extra day's worth of food in your backpack in case of an emergency.) Studying the Handbook to identify services and food sources at road crossings, or near the trail, that can be used can further reduce the amount of food in your backpack. If you are resupplying at shorter intervals, you will need to master the ability of picking up supplies and heading back on the trail without taking a full day off the trail. Unless you live to cook, stay away from the fancy gadgets and devices for preparing tasty meals on the trail that outfitters and hiking magazines love to tout. You do not need them, and they only add pack weight. You really do not have to worry about making food taste good on the trail. Whatever you prepare will taste great and you will not be able to get enough of it.

COMPASS AND NAVIGATIONAL AIDS

You do not need extraordinary map and compass skills to hike the Appalachian Trail; however, you should carry both in case of emergencies. For the most part the Appalachian Trail is well marked with white blazes (small white rectangles painted on trees, rocks and signs), and your only navigational requirement will be to follow the white blazes. Side trails are marked with blue blazes.

It is possible to miss a blaze and end up off the trail. If you find yourself hiking without seeing a white blaze for several minutes, you need to make sure you did not make a wrong turn. The first thing to do is to turn around to see if you can see a white blaze marking the trail for hikers going in the other direction. If you can see a white blaze, it is safe to continue in the direction you were going. If you cannot see a blaze, you should turn around and hike back until you can find a white blaze. When you reach a white blaze you can then figure out which way to go. If you reach a junction and are not certain of which way to go, a map and compass will come in handy.

If you are not paying attention, it is possible to wander completely off the trail. That happened to me once. The trail

A white blaze on the Georgia-North Carolina border.

was working its way up from a road crossing through some large rocks. I missed a switchback and continued through the rocks. When I realized that I was not on the trail, I tried climbing up the side of the mountain hoping to find the trail.

I was not finding the trail and the mountain was getting higher in the direction I was going. At that point I pulled out the map to get an idea of the terrain and where the trail might be. I decided to get out of the rocky area and found my way to the trees. Once I reached the trees, I carefully worked my way down to the side of the mountain. The slope was very steep, and I literally slid from tree to tree to keep from falling down the side of the mountain. When I reached a watercourse, I used a compass to determine which direction it was flowing. That gave me a general idea of where I was. I then followed the stream to a dirt road. At the road I used the compass to point me in the right direction.

Rather than being afraid or worried when I discovered I was off the trail, I realized that I was in a bit of a fix and that it was my job at that moment was to get out of it. There is really nothing to be afraid of—you have your gear to provide warmth and shelter; you have food to keep you from starving; and you have a map and a compass. All you need to do is to get to a point that you recognize to pick up the hike again. Until you reach a recognizable point, your best bet is to think of yourself as wondering how a novel with you as the lead character is going to end. You also owe it to those who care about you and depend upon you to get out of this jam successfully. Losing your wits and not succeeding is not an acceptable option.

OTHER EQUIPMENT ITEMS

In going on a long distance hike, there are some items that you will want to carry that you would not necessarily take on a shorter hike. If your glasses tend to loosen—you will want to take a small screwdriver for tightening them up. You may even want to take a back-up pair of glasses. Because you will be travelling to towns you will probably feel more comfortable with some personal grooming items such as deodorant. The combination of sweat, synthetic fabrics and infrequent showers is a highly potent combination. You will want to do whatever you can to modify your fragrance when in the company of non-hikers. Otherwise, you will see a massive evacuation as you enter a room.

Also as a long distance hiker, you will need to carry sufficient business materials (checks, address books and the like) to keep up with your off-trail responsibilities. If you really need to keep in touch, you may want to carry a cell phone. If you do carry a phone, please do not use it in camping areas or other areas where you will be invasive. The last thing the trail needs is to become an extension of a shopping mall or an airport terminal.

In the early part of the hike, when it is still cold, you will not need insect repellent or sunscreen. When you first start encountering insects, you can use a citronella based product to keep them away. As the insect season progresses you will want to switch to a real insect repellent—high strength deet. When I hiked the Appalachian Trail, the West Nile Virus was not the issue that it is today, but by using deet you will keep the virus-bearing mosquitoes away from you.

On some parts of the trail you will have to watch for deer ticks. They are the size of a freckle and can carry Lyme disease. The good news is that they need to chew on you for over a day before the disease is transmitted. If you find the tick before it has transmitted the disease, you should not have a problem. An evening body check for ticks should, therefore, become part of your daily routine. There will usually be notices posted where Lyme disease is a concern.

You can further reduce weight by only carrying the maps, and pages from the Handbook and Data Book that you are currently using. I even did the same with my reading material by cutting up Tolstoy's *War and Peace* (my trail reading project) into several sections. Essentially you will want to reduce weight wherever you can find it. Whatever you can shed will be worth it.

What You Will Not Need

Surprisingly, I discovered that I did not need a candle lantern. This is because when most thru-hikers begin their hike the days are already over twelve hours long and getting longer. In the first few weeks of hiking you will be so tired by the time you reach camp that you will be ready to go to sleep well before the sun completely disappears. However, if you will be hiking in the fall or winter, when the days are shorter, you will need some form of lighting.

CHAPTER
THREE

On the Hike

SUSTAINING THE HIKE AND PLANNING THE DETAILS

The general plan will have been made before you start your hike. Detail planning will occur throughout the hike every time you resupply. Like the general plan, detail planning will involve the trail maps, Handbook and Data Book. The primary reason for making a detail plan is to determine how much food to obtain at the resupply point. The first step in the detail plan will be to identify the next practical resupply point and how many days it will take to hike there. This will determine how many breakfasts, lunches, dinners and snacks will be required. You may be able to reduce the amount of food carried if there is a place to eat or a place to pick up something along the way. The Handbook will tell you everything you need to know about finding food and other support along the trail.

There are two ways hikers tend to resupply themselves. One is through mail drops and the other is to purchase items along the way. A mail drop is where you have someone mail a package to you in care of general delivery at a particular post office, or some other place (motel, store...), on your route. The Handbook identifies all of the post offices with their ZIP codes along the trail. The Handbook also identifies business establishments that will take mail drops. You will find that post offices in small towns are very efficient and that mail drops work very well. The post office will hold a package for two weeks. This means that it is important that the package be shipped at the right time — not too early or too late. Additionally, the post office will only accept packages that have been mailed — that is, no UPS or FedEx. You can only use UPS and FedEx for drops going to business establishments or personal residences.

A disadvantage of using mail drops is that you will need to do more detailed planning upfront to determine where to send mail drops and what to pack into each box. This also requires that someone take a very active role in supporting your hike by storing the boxes and making sure they get mailed in time to reach you. As a hiker, it means that you need to adhere to a schedule and make sure that you reach town when the post office is open. If you reach town just as the post office is closing on Saturday, you will end up waiting until Monday to pick up your drop.

Purchasing supplies as you travel along will give you more flexibility. When you factor in the cost of postage, purchasing as you travel along may not be any more expensive than buying your food ahead of time and mailing it. The disadvantage of purchasing as you travel is that you may not find what you want along the way. Many small country stores specialize in a limited selection of overpriced and out of date merchandise. I once spotted a package of cream cheese in a small market that was eight months out of date. You may want to use a combination of purchasing and mailing.

Regardless of how you resupply your food, you can save pack weight by using the mails for support items. When you are hiking in Georgia you will not need the maps for New

Hampshire or Maine. You can set up mail pouches for maps and have them sent to you as you move up the trail. As mentioned earlier, I cut my Handbook and reading material into sections and only carried the pages I was currently using. These items went into the same mail pouches as the maps. You could also set up mail drops for back-up hiking boots, replacement clothes, summer gear and other items such as water filter cartridges.

I created a "bounce box" for sundry and support items. The bounce box contained extra personal care items (deodorant, razor, shampoo...), water filter cartridges, boot wax, repair kits, cell phone battery charger, check book and various business items. There were enough items in the bounce box to handle most on-trail and off-trail situations. The bounce box bounced along the trail through the mails while I hiked. When I reached a town, I would pick up the bounce box at the post office. When I was done with the box and removed what I needed, I took it back to the post office and mailed it a week or so up the trail. The same concept can be used with gear that you are not using. If you are not certain if you should ship an item home permanently, or will not be using an item temporarily, you can mail it up the trail rather than carry it. When you catch up with the box you can then determine where to direct the gear. I was able to use the mails to alternate between my high-cut and low-cut hiking books based upon the expected terrain—which I was able to decipher from the Handbook, trail maps and talking to other hikers. I even met a hiker who would pack "town" clothes (blue jeans and comfortable shirt) in a bounce box. That way he was able to get out of his hiking clothes and wear something fresh while in town. You will be wise to use the post office as a resource to help you manage your hike with the least amount of pack weight.

As an older long distance hiker you will probably have some business that you will need to keep on top of back home. Business could range from as little as an occasional hello, to keeping the bills current, or actually performing business/money-making chores. Where most long distance hikers would only benefit from a cell phone in an emergency, a person actually conducting business could find it a handy tool. I was able to keep on top of several investment transactions with my cell phone while on the trail. Regardless of how you make phone calls you will need to have a good notebook with all the necessary details (phone numbers, addresses, account numbers and the like) to manage your life away from home.

If there is no one back home to pay the bills or to ship important mail to you, you will need to find a way to keep current with your obligations. My mother-in-law was able to handle the mail drops for my map pouches and gear boxes, but she did not have access to my personal mail. For that, I changed my address to a Mail Boxes Etc. (MBE). Every two weeks or so I would contact MBE and ask them to box up my mail and ship it to where I expected to be. It was the same as another mail drop. Sometimes I would get to my mail drop location and there would be a pouch from my mother-in-law, the bounce box and a box of mail from Mail Boxes Etc. All I needed was a Christmas tree to stash the boxes under.

WHILE ON THE TRAIL

When you step on the trail, it should be with a sense of gratitude to the visionaries who urged its development, the doers who actually put it on the ground and the many people who have kept it going. The least you can do is to develop an attitude of respect to the trail and others around you. This starts with following the guidelines of the "Leave No Trace" hiking and camping ethic. This means leaving absolutely no litter and carrying out your trash. Shoving trash into a fire pit for subsequent campers to burn is unacceptable. Trash is light; carry it out. This also means protecting the trail by staying on the trail even where it is wet. Short-cut paths and trail widening are not good improvements. Respect also applies to your conduct around other hikers. Invasive behavior is rude and unacceptable. Shelters are not the place for loud music, beer parties or cell phone use. If you want to party, stay in town. If you need to make a call, do it in private. If you have a dog, and I do, make sure that he or she is not bothering other campers. Respect also applies to your relationship to the rest of the world. You are not a hero just because you are hiking the Appalachian Trail. You are not owed "trail magic" (unsolicited favors), supplies if you are not prepared, or a place in the shelter just because you do not feel like setting up your tent. Respect will improve the trail experience for you and those around you.

You will develop routines while you are on the trail. When you stop to make camp, you will need to filter water, set up your tent, hang your clothes to dry, prepare dinner, clean-up, hang your food, update your journal, plan the next day, read and go to sleep. For planning the next day you will want to use your map and Data Book to determine how far you expect to hike the next day and where you will be able to get water. You will want to make sure that you make adequate progress each day in order to reach your resupply point before your food runs out.

In the morning you will have another routine of making breakfast, taking down your tent, packing your backpack, and erasing any signs of your being there. Make sure you have picked up everything. I must have left my rope behind four times while on the trail.

If it looks like rain, make sure your rain gear is easily accessible. If you are hiking and it does rain, you will want to have a good idea of the location of upcoming shelters in order to know where you can sit out a deluge. If you are hiking and there is lightning, you will want to make sure that you get out of exposed country as soon as possible. You will want to learn how to exercise your judgement between prudence and progress in hiking in rainy weather. It makes sense to sit out a downpour and lightning, while proceeding in light to medium rain or breaks in the deluge. If it is really bad, you may want to make camp early or take a well-deserved rest day in town.

WHEN YOU GET TO TOWN

You will eventually develop a routine when you get to town and will find those days busier than you expect. Obviously, your first task will be to find a place to stay and to take a shower. The Handbook is the best source for information on hostels, motels and other places to stay. After you are clean you will need to plan the next section (see "Sustaining the Hike" on page 39) to determine necessary purchases. You will also want to get to the post office before it closes. After that you can shop and do the laundry. Again, the Handbook will help with this. Because I was carrying very few clothes and I wanted them all washed, I carried a pair of running shorts for wearing around in camp and while doing the laundry. I would wear my rain jacket while my shirts (or shirt) were being washed.

After shopping you will want to repackage your food. You will become very familiar with the use of zip lock bags. To keep your pack weight down, you will want to measure out the exact amount of food you will consume on the next section. That is, if your next section will be four days and you drink one quart of Gatorade each day, measure out four or five quarts of Gatorade powder into a zip lock bag. If you have any left over, you can give it to another hiker, or put it in your bounce box and send it up the trail.

Town time is also a good time to clean gear, wax boots and make required repairs. If you are processing mail, you can write checks and respond to correspondence. Before the post office closes you will want to ship the bounce box up the trail, send any unnecessary gear home and send out mail. After taking care of business you can relax—check emails at the local library, pig out, or just rest.

1

CHAPTER
FOUR

The Hike Itself

It will still be very early spring when you start in Georgia.

THE HIKE ITSELF

If you are starting a thru-hike in late March or early April, it will still be very early spring (actually, late winter on the Appalachian Trail). There will be no leaves on the trees, the light will be stark and it can get cold. I even ran into snow in the Smokies in mid-April. The cold is not hard to deal with because when you are hiking you will warm up quickly and will soon be peeling off clothes. What is harder to deal with is rain and then more rain. The southern Appalachian Mountains are literally a cold weather rain forest. There is so much rain that the rhododendrons are trees rather than being normal bushes. If you care about making your goal and achieving what you expect from the hike, you will have to learn how to deal with the rain. You do not have to like it, but because there is nothing you can do about it, your best bet is to hang in there and keep pushing.

The hiking will be much harder than you expect. Even though no point on the Appalachian Trail in Georgia reaches as high as 4,500 feet or dips as low as 2,500 feet and the differences between peaks and valleys are usually less than 1,000 feet, the trail in Georgia is very rugged and choppy. You will feel like you are hiking on a roller coaster. Initially you will be on pace that will get you to Maine by never. But because you stay with it you get stronger and make progress. Eventually those ups and downs will no longer be a problem.

One of the things you can do to prevent the hike from becoming a never-ending walk on a treadmill through a green tunnel is to take advantage of your reduced pace to observe. If you do, you will notice changes in the light, the pick-up of a breeze and the skittering of a creature. You will notice how each day is different—a slight change in the temperature or of the exposure of a mountainside will completely alter the character of the trail. One stretch will be covered with small flowers and butterflies while a few hundred feet further up on the other side of the mountain there will be thousands of grasshoppers stirring up downed leaves as if they were making popcorn. You notice these because you have slowed your pace to allow yourself to experience the present. Even when these opportunities last only a second you will remember them long after you leave the trail, and all the struggles you go through will become worthwhile.

The first sign of real progress is when you leave the state of Georgia and cross into North Carolina. The mountains there are starting to get higher and the Smokies on the Tennessee—North Carolina border will be the highest of the entire Appalachian Trail, topping out at over 6,600 feet on Clingman's Dome. You will also start to encounter one of the most interesting landscape features on the Appalachian Trail—the southern balds. The southern balds are mountaintops that are clear of trees. Unlike the higher elevations of the west, or in New Hampshire, the "southern balds" are well below the meteorological timberline—they should have trees like the other mountains around them. There are many theories on why the balds exist. They range from being ice age remnants when the mountaintops would have been covered with ice, or having been cleared by Indians or early settlers. There is no consensus.

Siler Bald, North Carolina.

North of the Smokies you can visit the hot springs (in Hot Springs, North Carolina) that brought my wife and me to the Appalachian Trail in the first place. As you continue north, the cold weather will start to let up and buds begin appearing. With the buds the number of animals will increase. Most of the life you will see will be little life — insects, toads and efts. Be patient, you will have plenty of opportunities to see larger life — small mammals, bears and deer. I encountered all types of life (including bears, moose and poisonous snakes) and never had a problem. If you act in a non-threatening "just passing through" manner, I do not think you will have problems. I once came upon a mother bear and her cub. The mother sent the cub up a tree, stood by the base of the tree and waited to see what I would do. I kept walking. I did not stop to take a picture and spook the bear with flash, nor did I do anything else that could be construed as threatening. I felt honored to be able to see them, and made it clear that I was just passing through and would soon be gone.

When you reach Virginia, it will still not quite be spring, but spring will be trying to burst out with the buds now showing traces of leaves. There will still be some higher elevations when you come into Virginia. There will even be a stretch with wild ponies. As you move up Virginia the elevations begin to drop and all of a sudden you will be in the middle of spring. There will be flowers everywhere and the trees and shrubs will be completely bushed out. One week later it will be summer and you will start to swelter. This is the time to really reduce your pack weight by sending your winter items home.

You soon reach Shenandoah National Park. Many hikers like the park because there are so many opportunities to eat at restaurants near the trail. Some hikers were able to eat at a restaurant for both lunch and dinner. I did not care for the park because of the continuous road crossings, crowds, and diseased trees (from acid rain and gypsy moths). What is nice about the park is that for most hikers it is the first opportunity to see bears. The Smokies also have an abundance of bears, but when you will be hiking there it will still be cold and they may not be active.

North of Shenandoah National Park, you will leave Virginia and reach Harpers Ferry, West Virginia — the home of the ATC and the psychological halfway mark of the trail. The actual half way point is further north in Pennsylvania. You will have spent more time in Virginia than any other state, since close to one fourth of the trail is in Virginia.

You will also notice that many of the people you had been hiking with earlier on the trail are gone. Some of them only intended to hike a section. Others have left earlier than they

Appalachian Trail Conference Headquarters—Harpers Ferry, West Virginia.

planned. Typically only 15 percent of those intending to hike from Georgia to Maine actually complete the hike. Some drop off because they hurt themselves. The best way to avoid hurting yourself, especially for the older hiker, is to start off slow and to rest when appropriate. Most drop off because they could no longer mentally handle the hike. (Mentally handling the hike is less of a problem for the older hiker, because many of the older hikers appreciate the calm found on the trail.) In Bill Bryson's book he was afraid of bears and obsessed with the difficulties. He convinced himself that he could not make it to the end. It was easy to tell when someone was getting ready to leave the trail. They would start talking about things that they did not have on the trail—friends, comforts, food, school or something else that was moving them mentally away from the trail. Even if they did not admit it, they were really saying that they did not want to be on the trail anymore. You basically could start the countdown clock on their leaving. In my case,

I liked the food I was eating, did not miss anything and really did not want to be anywhere else than hiking the trail.

As you leave Harpers Ferry you will cross over the Potomac on an old railroad bridge. Once in Maryland, you will follow the towpath of the historic Chesapeake and Ohio Canal and soon will be on South Mountain passing through the outskirts of Antietam Battlefield — the site of the bloodiest day of the Civil War. Very quickly you will be in Pennsylvania. You will continue to see historic sites as you pass old iron forges. After one of the forges you will be at the actual halfway point of the trail. Instead of counting up you will now be counting down. You are no longer thinking of how far you have come but how little there is to go — still almost 1,100 miles.

Pennsylvania has a reputation for being rocky, but by the time you reach Pennsylvania you will be flying and making great time despite the rocks. You will learn to go over rocks rather than through them. You will have the opportunity in northeastern Pennsylvania to hike through an environmental disaster area and designated "superfund" clean-up site at Lehigh Gap. Right about the time you reach Lehigh Gap you will begin to see wild blueberries. They are delicious, and you will find them all the way to the end of the trail. You will also add several, and very worthwhile, days to your hike from spending much of the day bending over to gather them up.

Soon you will cross the Delaware River and enter New Jersey. Where you spent over a month in Virginia, you will now be passing through multiple states in a matter of weeks. Where you had once been struggling, you are now at peak strength with a lighter pack and clipping off the miles. You now have less than 900 miles to go, and are thinking it should be a snap.

In New Jersey the trail works it way around the northwest corner of the state — not too far from the huge metropolitan

Environmental "superfund" site near Lehigh Gap, Pennsylvania.

area of New York. You will see more wildlife (read bears) in New Jersey than anywhere else on the trail. I was fortunate enough to share the trail with four bears in two days and heard several more scamper in the brush. You will also start to encounter glacial ponds and other remnants of ice age activity. You will be frequenting ponds all the way to the end of the trail. You will also have stretches of swamps in New Jersey. The insects will be so intense there that you will not be able to stop for a rest and will even be tempted to run. At this point you will start using full strength deet (insect repellent) for the balance of the hike. Some day an entrepreneur will make a fortune by inventing a hiking helmet that will put out a steady mist of deet.

After being in New Jersey for only a few days, you will reach New York. I was expecting a nice gentle cake-walk to the Hudson River. It's not. It is a rugged section of climbing over one rock ridge after another. On one of the ridges you have an unobstructed view of Manhattan skyscrapers less than 35

New Jersey swamp—enter with deet.

miles away. I was fortunate to cross that ridge on a very clear day and had a great view. Surprisingly, even though the largest city in the country is so close, this was one of the most deserted sections of the trail.

When you cross the Hudson River on the Bear Mountain Bridge, you will be at the lowest point of elevation on the trail. East of the Hudson River it will begin to have a New England feel. You will be crossing many abandoned stone fences. The old stone fences are a reminder that the dense forest around you was not always here. One hundred and fifty years ago most of the land on the eastern seaboard was divided into small farms—even rugged mountainsides had farmsteads. As better land became available elsewhere and farming techniques improved, less desirable farmland (on or near the mountains) was abandoned and reclaimed by forest. Throughout the trail you will discover traces and remnants of farmsteads and orchards.

You will quickly be in Connecticut, Massachusetts and Vermont. In Connecticut and Massachusetts you will not be

Church and burial yard—Lennox, Massachusetts.

in an economically marginal rural area. You will be passing through or near some very affluent and extremely "cute" ex-urban and vacation communities (outer reaches of New York and Boston). These are classic New England towns with Congregational churches, beautiful trees and small shops — right out of a picture book. In Vermont you will be following the route of the Long Trail, which is older than the Appalachian Trail, through the Green Mountains. The Green Mountains are in many ways an elevated wetland with many ponds and swamps.

At Mount Killington in Vermont you will hang a right to leave the Long Trail and will soon be in New Hampshire with less than 450 miles to go. Since Virginia you have been flying along and almost getting cocky with your ability to clip off miles. The White Mountains of New Hampshire will cure you of any illusions of invincibility. They are rugged and much tougher than what you have been hiking. Your daily mileage will plummet. When you get to the ridgelines, they will be crowded with tourists. When you look at your map you will see that there are easy ways and hard ways to get to the ridgelines. The Appalachian Trail takes the hard way, while the tourist hikers take the easy way. You will also be going through some of the most dramatic scenery of the trail, but in many ways as a thru-hiker you will feel out of place with all the tourists.

If you want, you can plan your hike around using the White Mountain huts. The huts are rustic lodges regularly spaced out along the trail that provide dinner and breakfast, along with a cot for sleeping. While they offer sleeping and meal accommodations, they do not have showers. Thru-hikers can oftentimes stay at the huts at no charge by helping out with the cooking and clean up. If you can work it out, the only

The tourists come up to Franconia Ridge White Mountains, New Hampshire *by an easier route than you will.*

Ten minutes later they will be gone and you will have the trail to yourself again.

food you would need to carry in the Whites would be snacks and lunch.

When you clear the White Mountains you have finally reached Maine. If you reach Maine in the second half of August, you will start having some cool weather again. Don't worry you will still have some sweltering days. One day in Maine it was so hot that I drank seven quarts of water and wrung out my bandanna and tee shirt several times during the day. You may want to make arrangements to have your cooler weather gear shipped back to you. Gorham, the last town in New Hampshire, is a good place to make this transition. You will also begin to see signs of fall with some of the trees starting to change colors. Those reaching Maine after mid-September will be hiking in full fall.

Maine is absolutely awesome. I cannot emphasize enough how awesome Maine is. If you only have time for a short section of the Appalachian Trail, I would recommend that you hike Maine. The tourists are gone, and you are back with hikers. The trail is rugged, but when you get to the mountaintops you have uninterrupted, unending views of mountains, ponds and trees. The forest floor is rugged with roots the thickness of your thigh tangled in the rocks. Moose, which actually became evident in Vermont and New Hampshire, become abundant in Maine. Almost every pond will have several moose. One morning I counted twelve moose in my first hour of hiking. You are at this point travelling with mixed emotions, one says to slow down and enjoy this wonderful area. The other says you are almost to the end and let's rush to get there.

One day you will reach a ridge top and will see off in a distance a massive mountain rising over 4,000 feet above the surrounding flatlands. It is the largest uplift of the entire trail. It is Mount Katahdin. It is what you have been focused on

The Trail in Maine.

Mount Katahdin, Maine.

since you first stepped on to the trail back in Georgia. Your emotional debate is over; you have seen the goal and want it. In a few days you will be there. It is actually one of the hardest climbs of the trail. You will not notice the struggle as you reach the sign on top of Mount Katahdin to conclude one of the greatest journeys of your life. It will be with mixed emotions that you will return down the mountain to conclude your hike.

Henry David Thoreau probably said it best in his book *Walden* when he left Walden Pond after living there for two years — *"I left the woods for as good a reason as I went there. Perhaps it seemed to me that I had several more lives to live, and could not spare any more time for that one.... I learned this, at least, by my experiment: that if one advances confidently in the direction of his dreams, and endeavors to live the way which he has imagined, he will meet with a success unexpected in common hours."*

You have been going through a punishing routine for the

last several months. By the time you reach the end, despite eating everything in sight especially when in town, you will have lost considerable weight. There is really no way for most people to eat as many calories as they are burning, although women do a better job of protecting their weight than men. Certainly one of the benefits of the hike is being able to eat as much of what you want without qualms. But, the weight loss and continuous exertion have taken their toll. Like a major league baseball player at the end of the season, you are dragging and, without knowing it, crabby. New Hampshire hitting you like a brick wall just as you are heading for home only adds to the fatigue.

If you are comfortable with not doing your hike in a continuous sequence, you may want to consider a flip-flop when you reach the Delaware River on the Pennsylvania — New Jersey border. A flip-flop is stopping at a point (in this case the Delaware River), taking some form of transportation to the other end of the trail (in this case Mount Katahdin) and hiking back to where you left off (the Delaware River). Using this strategy, you will be hiking the rugged sections of Maine and New Hampshire when you are still at peak strength; therefore they should take less out of you. (As an older hiker, you may need all the help you can get.) You will then be finishing on easier terrain, and perhaps, if you are lucky, cross the swamps of New Jersey when there are fewer insects. Again, if you wish to proceed in one continuous sequence, you just need to recognize that it will have some difficulty.

PEOPLE AND CULTURE OF THE TRAIL

You will meet other people on the trail and the resulting community, for most, is a pleasant surprise. Hikers come from all different cultural and economic backgrounds, but on the trail these mean nothing and differences evaporate because everyone is sharing the same goal. Because there is room for all and no need for competition, there is an atmosphere of total cooperation and acceptance.

An unusual quirk of the trail is the use by most long distance hikers of a trail name. Trail names are very similar to the names that people adopt on Internet bulletin boards. It is a way of establishing an identity and camaraderie without taking on too much intimacy. They are not mandatory, and being a party pooper I only used my first name. I was surprised that you do become comfortable with calling someone MUTTONHEAD or RED STAG.

Some of the people you meet on the trail will be very interesting to you, and you will seek them out. There are some people that you will meet for only one night that you will not forget. One of ours was an Australian in his fifties adventure travelling across America. The first leg of his adventure was a kayak trip across New York harbor and up a canal in New Jersey. From New Jersey he rode his bike to southwest Virginia to pick up the Appalachian Trail in Damascus, Virginia. I met him three nights south of Damascus as he was proceeding south on his 450-mile hike to Georgia. When he reached Georgia he planned to ride his bike to Minnesota, kayak down the Mississippi River from Minnesota to New Orleans, and ride his bike west from New Orleans to California. He then planned to conclude his trip with a hike of the John Muir Trail (200 plus miles), and a several hundred mile bike ride from Yosemite National Park to Los Angeles.

Even though you will meet many people, you will have the trail to yourself for most of the day. You will meet most people at night when you make camp. The trail community centers on the shelters because that is where most hikers, even those in tents, spend the night. If you do not want company, you can stay pretty much to yourself. There are very few camping restrictions on the Appalachian Trail. I camped as much away from the shelters as I did near the shelters.

If you are interested, all of the shelters have registers for hikers to record their thoughts and to leave messages. This will expand your hiking community to those not only in your immediate proximity but also to those ahead of you through their journal postings. You may have hiked with some of them before they pulled ahead of you, while others could have always been ahead of you. Who knows how many behind you consider you to be part of their community through your register postings?

Trail Magic (birthday party) at Stecoah Gap, North Carolina.

Also part of the hiking community, and another very pleasant surprise, are "trail angels" and "trail magic." "Trail angels" are providers of unsolicited goodwill and favors for hikers. "Trail magic" is what they dispense. Many of them are former hikers who wanted to do something in return for the favors done for them. Others were just interested in helping. Oftentimes you will cross a road and someone will be there handing out snacks and cold drinks. Sometimes you will stumble on an ice chest in the middle of the woods full of cold drinks with a sign that says "Hikers Help Yourselves." At one road crossing there was a man who wanted to spend his birthday with hikers. He had driven 90 miles on a very cold windy day to set up a birthday spread on a picnic table and gave every passing hiker a meal of hot dogs, cole slaw, potato chips, soda and birthday cake. The good will and surprises continued all the way from Georgia to Maine. It is an experience that you will find nowhere else and restores your faith in the potential goodness of people.

SAFETY

The question of safety on the Appalachian Trail will be brought up to you before you begin your hike. The reality is that very few troublemakers will go to the effort of hiking several miles to cause mischief. The Appalachian Trail is safe, but like anywhere else serious crime has occurred on the trail. With that in mind you need to exercise some discretion in sharing your plans and storing your pack at restaurants and the like. The best way to remain safe is to avoid people, places and situations that do not make you comfortable. If you are not comfortable hiking by yourself, it will be easy to find partners of similar age to hike with during the thru-hiker season.

The ATC does sponsor ridge runners in the more heavily used portions of the trail. Ridge runners, many of whom are former thru-hikers, have the responsibility of hiking and staying in a section of a trail to look for and report problems. They are there to answer questions, make sure the trail is in good repair and to report suspicious behavior to local law enforcement agencies.

Even though a retired local sheriff, who once gave me a ride and who had never been on trail, suggested I carry a gun, I never ran into a situation where I felt in danger. The only strange situations that I ran into were a couple of shelters being used by non-hikers as temporary housing. In both cases I did not stay long and moved up the trail. Eventually a ranger or a ridge runner will request a semi-permanent occupier of a shelter to leave.

The bottom line is that safety on the trail will be an extremely unlikely deterrent to an excellent adventure on the Appalachian Trail.

COST OF THE HIKE

Various books on hiking will quote an amount of $1.00 per mile for the cost of a long distance hike. Other than giving you something to work with, I believe an arbitrary number of that nature is meaningless. The hike will cost a different amount for each hiker. Answering the question of how much will it cost to thru-hike the Appalachian Trail is very much like answering the question of how long is a piece of string. It depends.

The most significant and overwhelming cost of any adventure will be the opportunity cost of spending six or seven months on a long distance hike. That cost will have to be determined by each individual and will be predicated by the availability and desirability of other opportunities. In my case the opportunity **was** being on the Appalachian Trail; therefore, I did not consider forsaken wages as a cost.

While you are on the trail you will still have your normal infrastructure (home, vehicles, insurance, etc.) expenses for maintaining your existence. These are expenses that you would be incurring whether you were on the trail or not. Common sense dictates that you minimize these expenses as much as possible. If you are in a period of transition, you may want to store your possessions rather than maintain a home. If your house will be unoccupied while you are on the trail, you may want to look into home share, or temporary rental arrangement. If you will be storing your vehicle, you can have your insurance company suspend your automobile coverage. You will want to keep the "comprehensive" portion of your policy in effect in the event a tree falls on your car.

A long distance hike will require backpacking gear (see "What to Carry" on page 19). If you are starting at ground zero and do not have any backpacking equipment, you can expect to spend anywhere from $1,200 to $1,500. If you are extravagant you could spend more. You will lose or wear out some of the equipment on the trail, but most of it will be available for future adventures.

You will also have the cost of getting to the trail and getting home. Again this cost will vary by each hiker. Some people will be getting rides. Others will be doing a combination of public transportation and rides.

On the hike itself, you will have the cost of trail food, lodging in towns, restaurants in town, maintenance in towns (laundry, postage, phone calls), supplies, replacing broken or lost gear and, perhaps, taking a side trip. These costs will be determined by how long you will be on the trail, how long you will be in town and personal tastes. They would not be significantly different than hanging out at home where you would be eating, going to restaurants, going to events, and doing other things with your money. The costs of putting yourself on the trail is certainly much cheaper than if you were travelling overseas or driving around the country for the same amount of time. Sleeping in a tent, eating simple food and not shopping is a relatively inexpensive way to spend time. A closer look at the on trail expenses for planning purposes is as follows:

TRAIL FOOD AND SUPPLIES

The cost of food will depend upon personal choice and will have some variation on where it is purchased. I believe $60.00 to $70.00 per week is realistic. This would amount to $1,500 to $1,750 for six months on the trail.

LODGING IN TOWNS

This will be determined by how many nights you stay in town and where you stay. The Handbook has information on all types of accommodations ranging from hostels to motels. Some hostels are free while others have a nominal charge. In the South motels are much cheaper than the North. It is not difficult to find accommodations for less than $30.00 per night. Fortunately, in the North where motels are more expensive, there are boarding houses and other alternatives. If money is an issue, you do not have to go into town; you can stay on the trail and just go into town for supplies and an occasional shower. A better choice for saving money is to share a room with a fellow hiker. Assuming 22 town stays over a six-month hike, and half of them with a two nights stay, that would be lodging for 33 nights. An average cost of $10.00 would be a lodging expense of $330.00, while a $30.00 average would be $1,000.00.

Not all of the motels on the trail will be as whimsical as the Helendorfer Inn—Helen, Georgia.

FOOD AND OTHER TOWN EXPENSES

If you stay away from steak houses, you should be able to eat for a reasonable amount of money while in town. $10.00 to $15.00 per day is a workable average. At 33 days that would be $330.00 to $500.00. Also while in town you will do laundry, mail letters and the like. These costs will average around $10.00 per town visit, or $200.00 for the hike.

EXPENSE SUMMARY

Trail Food	$1,500	to	$1,750
Lodging	$ 330	to	$1,000
Restaurants	$ 330	to	$ 500
Expenses	$ 200	to	$ 200
Contingencies (Gear, Surprises)	$ 200	to	$ 550
TRAIL BUDGET	$2,560	to	$4,000

The numbers above are only an estimate and will vary based upon the choices you make. The bottom line is that if you are able to find the time to do the hike and have figured out how to support yourself for that period, the actual cost of being on the trail should not prevent you from embarking on this adventure.

OTHER WAYS OF LONG DISTANCE HIKING

Not every older hiker is capable of carrying a backpack day in and day out. For those who are interested in hiking the trail without the weight of a backpack there are alternatives. There are people who help hikers slack pack (hiking without a full backpack) from Georgia to Maine for a fee. If you are hiking with another hiker, you can slack pack by using your car. This involves dropping off one hiker at one end of the day's route, driving to the other end of the route and hiking back towards your partner. The hikers would then exchange the car keys when they meet on the trail. The hiker with the keys would then drive back to pick up the other hiker. This requires careful planning and making sure you do not drift off the trail and miss your partner. The most unusual avoidance of carrying a pack I encountered was an older gentleman travelling with his RV. (He not only did not want to carry a pack; he did not want to sleep in a tent.) He would park his RV at a trailhead; hike to the midpoint of a predetermined trail section; tie a piece of surveyor's tape to a branch; and hike back to his RV. On the following day he would drive to the other end of his section and hike back to the piece of surveyor's tape. He expected his adventure to take over two years, and when he finally finishes he will have hiked the trail twice.

ATTITUDE

Some of the hikers will not be treating the hike the same as you. Some will be taking short cuts or spending much of the hike on roads rather than on trails. Some will seem to specialize in avoiding the marked trail as much as possible. Others will travel from town to town as if going on a six-month pub crawl. Their actions may not be your style, but how someone else chooses to do their hike is really not your concern — it's their time and their dime. As an older hiker, you need to remind yourself that many of the younger hikers will have greater need for socialization than you will. You will have your hands full taking care of yourself, and any reaction you may have regarding others will only take away from your experience. Reacting to them will only be letting them impact your life. There will also be plenty of people that will have similar values as yours. There is an expression on the trail that holds true—hike your own hike.

Ultimately you are doing the hike for yourself. I chose to follow the trail as marked—that was my choice. I also took advantage of slack packing opportunities (provided by my wife) when I could—again that was my choice. There is no prize for completing the journey. No one will be on the top of Mount Katahdin with a bag of money to reward you for doing the hike in a certain way. You have done it for yourself, and if you leave the trail with the feeling of having been on an adventure of a lifetime, you have done it right.

Conclusion

I hope that this book has been helpful in your decision making and planning for a personal adventure. Whether you wish to go on a long distance hike on the Appalachian Trail or embark on some other adventure, my only advice is to quit making excuses and just do it. You will not regret it. As hard as any adventure may be physically, it really is the mental challenge that is the toughest. Sometimes you need a little reminder of why you are on an adventure to get you back on track.

My spirits reached their lowest in Shenandoah National Park. I did not like the crowds, road crossings and diseased trees. While I was camping in a campground at the park, a ten year old boy stopped by to ask if I was hiking the Appalachian Trail. When I replied yes, he said, "I thought so because your tent is so small." He then asked about the hike and how we lived. He then said, "You mean to say that you hike everyday and camp at a different location each night and will do it for the rest of the summer — that is so cool." It is so cool to be free and alive, and my spirits were never again in doubt.

I hope that when you go on your long distance hiking adventure that you enjoy it as much as I enjoyed mine. When you leave the trail it will certainly be with mixed emotions.

One part of you will look forward to new challenges, while another will long for the clarity of being on the trail. It will have a long lasting affect on you. In my case, I have kept in contact with people I met on the trail and check my journal regularly to see where I was on a certain day. I continue to be member of the ATC and look forward to each issue of the *Appalachian Trailway News* (a benefit of being a member). Because I do not live in the East, I cannot be a regular volunteer on the Appalachian Trail. I have, however, involved myself with a nearby trail by adopting a section of the Continental Divide Trail in New Mexico where I now live. Another effect the trail has had on me is that I have less patience for trivial uses of my time. If I am involved with something that is a poor use of my time, I will exit it as fast as I can. I now walk out of a movie I do not like rather than waste my time waiting for it to get better. As a compromise, I now bring a magazine with me to the theater to read in the lobby while my wife watches the movie to its end.

Good luck on all of your adventures and remember to keep your load light.

CONTACT THE AUTHOR
DAVID RYAN
612–889–9640

E-MAIL:
info@newmountainbooks.com

WEBSITE:
www.newmountainbooks.com

ORDERING INFORMATION
CALL-IN YOUR ORDER TO 612–889–9640

FAX: 928–222–0022

WRITE:
NEW MOUNTAIN BOOKS
13233 Executive Ridge Dr., NE
Albuquerque, NM 87112

OR E-MAIL:
info@newmountainbooks.com